This workbook Belongs to

_____

AVALON CARVER

ISBN: 979-8-34084266-4(Paperback)

Curriculum Creator: Darnell Bell
Front cover image and illustrations by Camila Sanchez
Book design and editorsby- Chelsea McElwee, Kimberly A. Morrow, and Camila Sanchez

Published by Avalon Carver Community Center in the United States of America.

Avalon Carver Community Center
4920 S. Avalon Blvd.
Los Angeles, CA. 90011

www.avalon-carver.org

THE
Table of Contents

SELF-IDENTITY DEVELOPMENT

BARACK OBAMA

...A Real Smart Man

The phrase "the brother knows his stuff" is often used in neighborhoods to describe someone who is highly intelligent and well-informed. This certainly applies to former President Barack Obama. He lived by the powerful words of Malcolm X, the legendary human rights activist, "Education is our passport to the future, for tomorrow belongs to the people who prepare for it today" (Malcolm X, 1964).

Obama took this message to heart early on. He didn't just go to school—he excelled. He attended some of the top schools in the world: Occidental College, Columbia University, and later earned a law degree from the prestigious Harvard Law School. He understood that education was his key to unlocking the future, so he worked hard, stayed focused, and got smarter every day.

On the next page in the spaces provided, now think about you. How important is education in your life? How do you see it shaping your future goals and dreams? Take some time to reflect on how the support of your parents, grandparents, friends, etc., may be pushing you to stay in school and crush it. Your future is yours to build—how will you use education to get there?

"Write Your Own History..."

Good leaders are not afraid to walk into the unknown. They don't wait for someone else to go first—they lead the way. True leaders trust their instincts and take bold risks, even when others think it's impossible. For example, as a student at Harvard Law School, Barack Obama entered a contest that many thought he was sure to lose. The contest determined who would become the President of the prestigious Harvard Law Review.

In 1991, Obama took on this tough challenge, competing against other super smart students. It was not just about writing, editing papers, or reviewing court cases—he had to prove himself to his peers, the very people he was competing against. And in the end, he made history by becoming the first African American President of the Harvard Law Review since its founding in 1887.

Unfortunately, many people let life's challenges hold them back from dreaming big. Some believe they can only go so far and are afraid to try something new or different. Others let negativity from "haters" convince them they can never achieve greatness.

But here's the real question: do you have the courage to dream big? Can you write your own history like Barack Obama did? We believe you can. We believe each of you is a potential history-maker. Now it's your turn—share your thoughts on your big dreams and why it's important to dream BIG.

_____

_____

_____

_____

_____

_____

_____

_____

_____

_____

_____

_____

_____

5

The Assertiveness of Maxine Waters

The Assertive Me

Assertiveness is a very important quality for a person to possess. For too many years, black people were afraid to be assertive and stand up for what they thought was right and owed to them. The Civil Rights Movement of the 1960's was very important because we began standing up as a people for what we thought was right and began challenging the values and social systems of this society that were designed to keep us down, oppressed, and inferior.

Maxine Waters displayed this same kind of quality as she created, discussed, and supported legislation in Sacramento and in Washington D.C. that effected black people and black communities. As a politician, assertiveness was an important quality; as a black politician, it was crucial.

In the spaces below, please share your opinions on the importance of being assertive - standing up for what you think is right or wrong regardless of the consequences. You may want to include examples of times when you thought you were being assertive in your story.

Stand Up
(Behavior)

As we go through life, we often find ourselves in situations where we have to "stand-up" for and defend something that we have done. As a black
 woman politician representing a black community in Los Angeles, Congresswoman Maxine Waters was constantly being assertive and defending
her many actions in the California Assembly and later in the U.S. Congress.

This activity requires you to think of a time when you got into trouble for something you did that was either not understood or misunderstood.
Please describe the situation completely, including what your behavior was, why you behaved the way you did, how others reacted to your behavior, how you defended yourself, and how the situation was resolved.

In Defense of Self

Many times, Maxine Waters had to defend and speak up for the black community and the special needs of black

youth on the floor of the State Assembly and in Congress. Many people still had very negative opinions and

values about black people and the black community, so it was very important that someone like a Maxine Waters was around to tell people what we are really like and to fight for the kinds of programs we needed to

improve our communities and our overall condition. Of course, Ms. Waters could have been silent and let all of

the negative things said about the black community go by unchallenged, but that was not her style. She is a very

assertive woman who will stand up for what is right, especially if it concerns black people.

In the spaces below, please describe a time when you had to verbally defend your family, friend, or community.

Please describe what took place in the situation, including what was said that made you react, how you reacted,

how you felt then and why you felt the way that you did, what did you say, how you felt afterward, etc.

The Devotion of Frederick Douglass

The Devoted Me

In the early days of America, Frederick Douglass, a free black man during the days of slavery, devoted his life to writing and lecturing against slavery. He often traveled to Europe to speak to groups about the "strange American institution", the evils and the immorality of men of one color owning, selling, and treating as property, men of another color. He often put himself in dangerous situations because of his devotion to helping his "brothers" get their freedom in this so-called "land of freedom".

When someone is devoted to another person, or to an idea, one really doesn't care or worry about the dangers, or bad things, they subject themselves to, or the dangers they might face because of this devotion.

This lesson requires you to write a story about a time when you were devoted to, or stood up for, another person or something that you believed in.

In your story, please describe who the person was or what the idea was that you stood up for; why it was so important for you to stand up for this

person or idea; how you felt doing what you did; how did the other person involved in the situation feel; what could have, or did, happen to you

because of your "stand"; etc.

It is easier
to build
strong children
than to repair
broken men

Sacrifices

In the early days of America, Frederick Douglass, a free black man during the days of slavery, devoted his life to writing and lecturing against slavery. He often traveled to Europe to speak to groups about the "strange American institution", the evils and the immorality of men of one color owning, selling, and treating as property, men of another color. He often put himself in dangerous situations because of his devotion in helping his "brothers" get their freedom in this so-called "land of freedom".

When someone is devoted to another person, or to an idea, one really doesn't care or worry about the dangers, or bad things, they subject themselves to, or the dangers they might face because of this devotion.

This lesson requires you to write a story about a time when you were devoted to, or stood up for, another person or something that you believed in.

In your story, please describe who the person was or what the idea was that you stood up for; why it was so important for you to stand up for this person or idea; how you felt doing what you did; how did the other person involved in the situation feel; what could have, or did, happen to you because of your "stand"; etc.

Community Service

Frederick Douglass believed in and was devoted to a free black community. He felt that it was his "mission" or "responsibility" to do all that he could to help his fellow black American obtain their freedom. His devotion led him to write a newspaper, The North Star, and to travel the world speaking out against slavery. Like Douglass, we also have a responsibility to the black community. Our lives should be devoted to improving the conditions in our communities and making them better places to live in.

This lesson requires you to list two things that you don't like in your community. After you list the two community problems, you will pick one of them and write a story about what you can do, or would like to do, to make your community "better". Make sure to talk about the problem, or thing you don't like. Discuss why the problem is a problem to you; how it effects the community; how do people feel about it; etc. Also, include what you would do to improve things in your community and the ways that the community would be changed because of you.

Two Things That I Don't Like Or Two Community Problems

1 _____

2 _____

_____

_____

_____

_____

_____

_____

_____

_____

_____

_____

The Eloquence of Jesse Jackson

The Persuasive Me

Jesse Jackson is a very eloquent and persuasive speaker. Just by talking, he is able to influence people to do different things. In 1984 and 1988, Jesse Jackson tried to become President of the United States. He formed a group made up of people from different races - The Rainbow Coalition - who supported and guided him in this very difficult quest. In his bid to become President, he had to go to many different cities and make speeches telling people why they should vote for him in the big presidential election. He didn't do too well in 1984, but things were a little better in 1988. He hoped that his speeches would be persuasive enough to influence people to vote for him because of his stand on issues, and not simply disregard him because of his color.

We have also been institutions where we tried to influence a friend, relative, or teacher. Sometime, we tried to influence others when we wanted to "get our way", get support from others, or in trying to get out of trouble. In the spaces below, describe a time when you tried to be persuasive, when you tried to influence the attitudes or behavior of another person. Be sure to include information in your story about what the situation was; why you wanted to influence the other person; how you influenced the other person; and so on.

The Spokesperson in Me

A spokesperson is someone who speaks up for, or represents a group of people. Sometimes, because someone may be a good, persuasive, convincing person who is able to express himself or herself well with words, they may be asked to say something to someone else on behalf of the group. To a number of people, Jesse Jackson is the spokesperson for Black Americans.

Jesse Jackson is regularly seen and heard on television, radio, and in newspapers speaking out against racism, economic oppression, and exploitation of black people in America and in Africa. He is constantly trying to raise the awareness of white America on the conditions encountered by Black Americans.

In this lesson, your are to describe a time when you had to speak up for your classmates, friends, or brothers and sisters. Don't forget to describe the situation as completely as possible.

It's Not What You Say, It's How You Say It

You know that old expression, "**It's not what you say, it's how you say it**", is really true. It seems that the tone of our voice that we use in talking to others is sometimes much more important than what we want or mean to talk about in the first place. Have you ever thought you were saying something nice to someone else, but they took it the wrong way because of the tone of your voice, or the way you said it? Sometimes, we can say good and nice things in a sarcastic way by accident, and the person we're talking to reacts in a very different way than we expect. Jesse Jackson was very much aware of the importance of **tone and body language** used in saying things.

Jesse proves that when you say something is sometimes just as important as what you say and how you say it. **Timing**, when you say something, is very important and can lead to very big misunderstandings. When Dr. King was assassinated, Jesse got into big trouble with the leadership of the Black Movement. It's not what he said that was wrong or bad after the assassination, but that he wasn't supposed to speak to the media in the first place.

The Reverend Ralph Abernathy, Dr. King's assistant, told everyone to be quiet and not talk to the press until they had a chance to meet.

However, Jesse did talk to the press while the others were meeting and became a national figure that day. He was called an "**opportunist**", but he felt that someone had to jump in and take charge. He did, and Reverend Abernathy didn't.

In the spaces below, you are going to describe a time when you said something that you meant in one way, that was taken a very different way by someone you were talking to. Discuss the reasons that might explain the misunderstanding and its effects upon you and the person you were talking to.

The Fearlessness of Bishop Desmond Tutu

The Brave Me

A lot of people are brave and very brave people are really fearless. I mean, to really be fearless, one has no fears; one is afraid of nothing. Desmond Tutu is a very brave person. After all, Bishop Tutu is black, speaks his mind on the inequalities black people experience, and is critical of the system of apartheid in South Africa which separates the races in the country. Maybe Bishop Tutu
does have his share of fears, but he realizes the importance of what he is trying to do in South Africa and sees what he's doing as worth the price "it could cost him".

A number of us are also brave. We have shown how brave we are by something we either did or said. Some of us may have stood up to someone bigger than we were or volunteered to do or say something in class in front of our classmates. Some of us have shown how brave we were by trying some of the scary rides at amusement parks.

In the spaces below, you are to write a story about a time when you were brave and showed people how courageous you were, either by doing something or saying something. Make sure that your story contains all of the facts.

Freedom at Any Cost

Bishop Tutu is a fearless man who believes in "freedom at any cost". This means that he feels that fighting for the freedom and equality of his fellow African

brothers and sisters is more important than being called names, insulted, beaten-up, and even being murdered. There have been many other black men and

women, here in America, who also have believed in freedom and equality at any cost. Many of these same black people were called names, insulted, put in

jails, and even assassinated. Dr. Martin Luther King was one such person.

Even though there have been many black men and women not afraid to speak out for the freedom and equality of their fellow black man, there still have not

been enough such people. It seems that too many of us get afraid of losing our reputation, our jobs, our friends, our homes, etc., and "chicken out" and do and

say nothing. A lot of us are not fearless when it comes to improving our communities. We get afraid and start making all kinds of excuses why we don't, or

can't, do certain things to improve our community. Perhaps, we should be like the Panthers of the 1960's, who set out to clean up their East Oakland

community. They put themselves on the line, took up guns, knives, and sticks and chased the dope dealers out. They were not afraid of dying.

In the spaces below, you are to describe a time when you may have risked your life to do or say something. If you have never risked your life to do or say something, use your imagination and write a story about the kinds of things you think you would risk your life for when you become an adult.

_____

_____

_____

_____

_____

_____

_____

_____

_____

_____

_____

_____

_____

And the Young Shall Lead

We all recognize how fearless the Bishop Desmond Tutu is. We see him risking his life every day in his hostile and dangerous homeland, South Africa, preaching to his brothers and sisters about equal rights and self-determination (being in charge of and controlling one's own destiny). This may seem a bit strange when one realizes that South Africa has more than 15 black Africans to every one white Afrikaner. While they outnumber white South Africans, black South Africans have no political or economic power in their own land.

Back in the 1960s, again during the Black Power Movement in America, fearless black warriors formed gangs to clean up the black community. These gangs consisted of the Black Panthers, the US, the Nation of Islam's Fruit of Islam, the Black Student Union, the Students Non-Violence Coordinating Committee, etc. These brothers made sure that drugs and dope dealers did not deal in the community. They didn't play; in other words, they fought fire with fire. If it took violence to chase the dope dealers out of the neighborhood, they would use violence. They were not afraid to use guns, bumper jacks, knives, etc., to deal with drugs and drug dealers. At times, they also had to go "toe to toe" with the police. Even though these fearless brothers were part of a gang, they were part of a gang that was trying to improve their communities.

In the spaces below, write a story about a gang of fearless young brothers and sisters who are trying to do good things for the community. Keep in mind that a gang is "only a group of people" and it can be good or bad.

_____

_____

_____

_____

_____

_____

_____

_____

_____

_____

_____

The Judgmental
Thurgood Marshall

Law & Order: Rules

Everyone knows what laws are...right? Laws are like rules that grown-ups
are supposed to follow. They are society's
way of letting us know what we can and cannot do. As a judge on the
United States Supreme Court, Thurgood Marshall
found himself in a very special situation. Thurgood Marshall, a black
man, was able to determine what things should and
should not have been laws and how these laws should have been
interpreted. He was in a position where he could play
"watch dog" and protect the rights of black people and women.

For this assignment, you will have to name some of the laws that you run
into at home, school, or in your neighborhoods.
I want you to give your opinion on the law; is it a good one, a bad one,
and why. Like all of these assignments, please go
into detail when you describe the law.

Less Fortunate Than Us

Everyone knows what laws are...right? Laws are like rules that grown-ups are supposed to follow. They are society's way of letting us know what we can and cannot do. As a judge on the United States Supreme Court, Thurgood Marshall found himself in a very special situation. Thurgood Marshall, a black man, was able to determine what things should and should not have been laws and how these laws should have been interpreted. He was in a position where he could play "watch dog" and protect the rights of black people and women.

For this assignment, you will have to name some of the laws that you run into at home, school, or in your neighborhoods. I want you to give your opinion on the law; is it a good one, a bad one, and why. Like all of these assignments, please go into detail when you describe the law.

We All Make Mistakes

Yes, we all make mistakes. It is a part of human nature for us to "mess up" or make the wrong decision every once in a while. But you know, some of us
seem to make a habit of doing or saying the wrong thing. Even though most mistakes are bad, sometimes, good things can come from them. Sometimes we
learn valuable lessons from our mistakes...lessons that can spare us from making future mistakes.

A number of big businesses and even State governments made mistakes in their interpretation of the Constitution as they tried to use it to justify their
discrimination and prejudice towards black people and women. However, after going to court and facing Thurgood Marshall, they learned that the
Constitution couldn't be used to "take rights away" from the less fortunate.

In the spaces below, you are to describe a big mistake that you once made. Make sure that your story includes facts about what your mistake was; what you
did wrong; what you should have done; why you did what you did; what were the consequences of your actions; and how did you feel about the mistake you
made.

The Magnificence of
MARCUS GARVEY

Visions Of A Better Place

Marcus Garvey dared to dream of a very special place. Garvey dreamed of a place where all black people could experience honor, dignity, respect, and hope. He knew, all too well, that America would never treat its black citizens with respect. To Garvey, America was not our home; it was a place that we were brought to as slaves. If we were going to live our lives with dignity, honor, and hope, we would have to return to OUR homeland; we would have to return to Africa. Garvey devoted his life, skills, and resources to getting us back to "the land of our forefathers."

Many of us dream of a better place to live. Sometimes, we dream about a different house, a different neighborhood, a different city, a different state, and even a different country. This activity asks you to describe that special place where you would like to live. Describe all of the reasons why this place is so special to you. Your story should include some of the things you would do at your special place that you can't do where you currently are, and the advantages (and disadvantages) of living there.

43

A Leader Of Men

Marcus Garvey was a charismatic leader who was supported by millions of black people in America. The "common" black man was impressed by his message of true respect and dignity for black Americans only being possible in their homeland, Africa. They were able to relate to, and accept, his suspicions of everything white, and his praise of everything black. They saw a man who not only was talking about his blackness, but a man who was also backing it up with actions. Garvey showed how serious he was by forming several black organizations. These organizations included the Universal Black Cross Nurses, the Universal African Motors Corporation, the Black Flying Eagles, and a newspaper, The Negro World.

Many of us have, one time or another, either served as leaders, or would have liked to be a leader. Some of us have been leaders in school, class, church, etc. Those who have served as leaders know that it isn't as easy job; many responsibilities come with the job. Sometimes, you may miss out on things, make enemies, and even lose friendships because of the decisions you must make as a leader.

This exercise requires you to describe your experiences as a leader. You are to describe what kinds of groups you have served as leader in; what kinds of things you did; what were your responsibilities; what you liked and disliked about the responsibility; and how you felt.

I Dared To Dream

Have you ever stared out of a window, or stared at the stars, and daydreamed about your future? Have you ever wondered what it will be like ten (10) years from now;
 where you will be living; how much money you'll have; who you will be married to.

Marcus Garvey was also a daydreamer. He dreamed of a country in which black people would be respected, treated equally, and could live with dignity and honor. He
 dreamed of leading black people home, back to Africa. Marcus Garvey did more than just daydream. He organized businesses, raised huge sums of money, and spoke
 around the country in an attempt to get other black people to join him in his effort to make his dream a reality.

This activity requires you to sit back and dream about your future. Look into that big crystal ball and see yourself ten (10) years from now. WHAT DO YOU SEE?

47

The Nationalism of
MALCOLM X

GROWING PAINS

One of Malcolm X's famous speeches dealt with the "The Ballot or the Bullet". The speech discuss the ways that he saw black people overcoming segregation and racial oppression. He felt that black people could exercise their political rights and effect change through voting or black people could "pick up the gun" and resort to violence to get what was rightfully theirs.

In his earlier years, Malcolm would have said that the bullet was the way. He was a young, angry, and impatient follower of the Black Muslims and saw no other way to deal with America. At this stage of his life, he considered all white people to be "devils".

As he matured, he began questioning many of the teachings of the Honorable Elijah Muhammad. He left the Muslims and started his own organization, the Organization of Afro-American Unity, in which he saw all men, regardless of color, as brothers. At this stage of his life, he was older, wiser, and would have chosen the ballot as the way to deal with American society.

As we have grown older, some of our beliefs have changed. This assignment requires you to look at something that you feel strongly about
now, that you didn't feel as strongly about earlier in your life. Make your story as complete as possible.

STAND TALL!!!

Brother Malcolm stood up for his beliefs and "stood tall" in the face of danger. He stood up for his beliefs and values, and often found himself at odds with Martin Luther King, Jr., the Honorable Elijah Muhammad, and American society, in general. Even though he knew that his beliefs were not widely accepted and could lead to his death, Malcolm X continued to say the kinds of things that the Black masses wanted to hear.

Sometimes at school, or at home, we have to stand up for something that we really believe to be right. Everyone around us, including our friends, teachers, and parents may think that we are "dead wrong", but we know deep In our hearts that we are right. Sometimes, we even get into trouble because of this belief.

On the next page, tell about a time when you really stood up for something that you thought was right. Tell what the situation involved; why you felt the way that you did; what happened to you for standing up; and how you felt afterwards.

MY NAME'S THE GAME

Our names tell a lot of things about us. We can usually figure someone out pretty well just by knowing their name. Names can sometimes be mirrors - reflecting important things about a person's values and personality. Malcolm X knew the importance of a person's name. Born as Malcolm Little, Malcolm's younger years were marked with problems related to his rebellious attitudes and "street" behavior. Detroit Red, his "street" nickname, was one of those "hardheaded, going nowhere, who would wind up in jail eventually, kids". Sure enough, the "street slick" Malcolm "was busted" and did serious time in jail.

However, a funny things happened to Malcolm in jail. He met other prisoners who followed the teachings of the Honorable Elijah Muhammad, and began reading and studying about the Black Muslims. As his knowledge and faith grew in "this new religion", his life took on a completely new meaning. He became "reborn". He began to understand his previous lifestyle and all of the mistakes he had made. He became more serious about being a part of the Black Muslim movement and helping other black people understand the "trick bag" that they were in and how to best "get out of it". He dropped his "slave name", his last name - Little, and began using "X" (for his unknown and stolen African last name). He was now an ex-slave...a new man with a new purpose. Later, as Malcolm continued to grow spiritually, he began his own black organization and changed his name again. He began calling himself El Shabazz Malik.

This exercise is actually a little game using adjectives that will reveal a lot of things about ourselves. You are going to write you name vertically on the chart which follows and then match adjectives (describing words) with the corresponding letters in your name that describe you. Try to be as honest as possible.

DOLORES HUERTA

A TIME TO ORGANIZE

Because its so very difficult- as one person- to bring about change, it is so important to learn how to organize other people who have similar concerns and mobilize them to take action. A well organized effort with passionate and committed participants has the potential of truly changing a situation that might seem unfair, unequal and "just wrong". The "Civil Rights Movement", the Black Lives Matter Movement", and the Grape Boycott were examples of community organization efforts designed to address a wrong.

Dolores Huerta loved working with people and organizations committed to making things better for people in the community; she was a very good organizer. In 1962, she co-founded the National Farm Workers Association with Cesar Chavez – an organization devoted to bettering the lives and wages of farm workers. In 1960, Huerta co-founded the Agricultural Workers Association which set up voter registration drives and pressured local governments for barrio improvement.

This activity asks you to think about your skills as an organizer and mobilizer; your ability to have friends and neighbors join you and change something, - a situation, a law, a disparity. First, you will have to identify an issue and then describe how you would organize/mobilize friends to change it.

DIVINE INTERVENTION

Do you consider yourself to be a lucky person? Many of us have been – or have friends and relatives who have been – in situations that could have had bad consequences. We, or people that we know, may have seen a car run a red light just before the car that we were riding in approached the intersection. We, or people that we know, may have been around someone throwing something dangerous into a crowd, and we were not harmed by the object...but others were. Old sayings like, "someone's got your back" or "divine intervention" are used to explain how lucky we may have been.

Dolores Huerta stood beside Robert F. Kennedy on a speaker's platform at the Ambassador Hotel in Los Angeles as he delivered a victory speech to his political supporters after winning the California Democratic Presidential Primary election in 1900. Only moments after the candidate finished his speech, Huerta was a safe distance behind Kennedy as he and five other people were wounded by gunfire inside of the hotel's kitchen area. If she had not moved from the group 15 minutes earlier, she would have been wounded and possibly murdered during the incident. Wow, she was surely lucky to have moved when she did.

In the spaces below, please describe a time when you, a friend, or relative may have had this same kind of luck and walked away from a dangerous situation safely.

WHAT I STAND FOR

Our lives are so very short and it is so important that we live our lives helping our children, our families, our friends and our communities. We must take the time to find a "cause" or an issue that is worth fighting for. Even though we may not seek it, we will be praised for our efforts if our lives are filled with "good works". Dolores Huerta devoted her life to helping improve conditions of farm workers.

In October 2010, Dolores Huerta was praised as "a lifetime champion of social justice whose courageous leadership created unprecedented national support for farm workers, women and underserved communities in a landmark quest for human and civil rights" by Mills College. She also received the Presidential Medal of Freedom from President Barack Obama on May 29, 2012.

Is there a "cause" or issue that you feel strongly about? In the spaces below, please write about something that you feel strongly about and that, even now, you can see devoting your life and future efforts toward.

61

CESAR CHAVEZ

THE ODDS WERE AGAINST YOU

Cesar Chavez was a very brave and courageous man. Cesar Chavez was a Mexican-American labor leader who used non-violent methods to fight for the rights of migrant farm workers in the southwestern USA. Migrant farm workers were people who did farm labor, moving from farm to farm and town to town as work was
needed. It was difficult work that paid very little and it was very dangerous because of the pesticides used by the farm owners.

As a labor organizer, Chavez would find himself in conflict with large farm and land owners who didn't care about their workers and were only interested in their work in the fields; they wanted their crops picked. These land owners were rich, wealthy and powerful people. Even though the odds were against him, Cesar Chavez did not back down.

In the space below, please describe a time when you accomplished something that was special even though the "odds were against you" and others thought that you couldn't do it.

OUTSIDE OF MY COMFORT ZONE

Doing something that you know can result in harm to you and to your family members requires courage. We all say that someone is brave and courageous when they stand up in the face of adversity and take on a challenge regardless of the consequences. We see someone who defends his brother and sister against a crowd of people as being brave. A fireman rushing into battle an out of control fire is considered to be brave. Someone who is afraid of large crowds, who gets the courage to grab a microphone to deliver a speech is acting bravely.

Cesar Chavez organized "strikes" (when workers refused to work until improved working conditions and salaries are met) and nationwide "boycotts" (protests in which the public is asked not to buy certain products). He did this knowing that he was putting his life and the lives of his family members at risk.

Though we may do things that don't endanger the lives of ourselves and those closest to us, we are all called upon to be brave and courageous; we all do things outside of our "comfort zone". In the space below, please describe a time when you did something that required you to be brave and show courage either in the classroom, at home, or around your friends.

66

Michelle Obama

Honesty

Honesty or truthfulness is a facet of moral character that connotes positive and virtuous attributes such as integrity, truthfulness, straightforwardness (including straightforwardness of conduct: earnestness), along with the absence of lying, cheating, theft, etc. Honesty also involves being trustworthy, loyal, fair, and sincere. Honesty is the key skill for anyone who wants to be inspiring millions and Michelle Obama has that. She has been dedicated to so many social causes. Her authenticity and honesty go for the win when it comes to bringing a change in society and standing up to what is correct and what is not. Her book, Becoming, is all about honesty. She described "the America I know and that so many marginalized people know. At times, inequality seems-, as American as apple pie. It is about instilling hope and optimism while maintaining honesty. Becoming is a reminder that America is still a work-in-progress, and that hope can be an action word if we allow it to be." Of course, she was accused of being anti-American by many Republicans who didn't appreciate her honesty, but their words didn't stop her from honestly expressing her opinions. Honesty is a character trait that we all value; everyone wants us to be honest with them about everything. We would think that everyone appreciates and respects our honesty, but this is not always the case. Just as many Republicans did not like Michelle's honest comments about the inequality in America, many of our friends and relatives get angry with us when we are "too honest." Sometimes, we have lost friendships/relationships because we were sometimes too honest. In the spaces below, please describe a situation in which your honesty had either bad or good results.

Graceful

Being graceful is about more than just not tripping over yourself. It's not only a way of carrying your body, but of maintaining control over your actions as well as your thoughts. People who are graceful are naturally elegant without being aloof, and they care for other people and treat them with respect. People who are graceful are also classy; they are confident and sure of yourself and know how to conduct themselves in any situation. Michelle Obama was described as being "a lioness who walks with grace. Her sense of dressing is more than just fashion. She is a very positive human and sticks to the facts and moves ahead with her idea of change she wishes to see in society." Consequently, she has been compared to Jacqueline Kennedy due to her sense of style, and also to Barbara Bush for her discipline and decorum.

We all have been in situations with friends, family, school and/or work associates that required us to be "graceful and classy." Sometimes, we find ourselves in disagreements and/or arguments, that require us to "take the higher road" and to respond in a nicer, calmer fashion so that we don't escalate the situation. Being graceful and classy in these situations is not easy and they require us to exercise discipline and self-control.

In the spaces below, describe a situation –disagreement, discussion or argument – that you found yourself in that required you to be the calm one and exercise grace and class.

Compassionate

Compassion is the ability to understand and share the feelings of others, and to act on that understanding in a way that helps alleviate their suffering. It is a social feeling that motivates people to go out of their way to relieve the physical, mental, or emotional pains of others and themselves. Being compassionate to people throughout the walk of life is always a plus in a person's personality and Michelle Obama excels here. Before she was the First Lady, she was a practicing lawyer and used to fight for her community's social issues. After this, she also established Chicago Chapter for public allies which is a social network that helps youth to prepare for civil services.

Michelle Obama wanted her work in the area of childhood obesity to be her legacy, something that people would remember her for. Like she said, "I want to leave something behind that we can say, 'Because of this time that this person spent here, this thing has changed.' And my hope is that that's going to be in the area of childhood obesity."

When we watch or listen to the news on television and radio, or on social media, we see tremendous suffering around us. Sometimes, when we're walking to school, work or just throughout the city and community, we see people, families and children suffering. Many of us see family members suffering. People with compassion "feel" the suffering of others, and are motivated to try to do something –big or small- to help.

In the spaces below, please describe how you feel when you see others suffering and what you have done, or would like to do, to help reduce their suffering.

Inspirational

Michelle Obama is an inspiration for many. Her never-ending efforts to fight against poverty, inequality and her urge to fight against transgender politics and racism. She has inspired many to change society and its thought process. Being inspirational refers to having the ability to inspire or motivate others to take action or make changes in their lives. It can mean being a role model, having a positive attitude, or being able to share wisdom and knowledge that helps others achieve their goals. Inspirational people can come from all walks of life and can inspire others in many different ways.

"Throughout my life, my mother has been one of my biggest role models. My mom didn't get to go to college. She didn't have a fancy job. But my mom had a lot of common sense, and she loved me and encouraged me through all the challenges that I faced." Inaddition to her mom, Michelle looked up to her older brother. "He kind of paved the way for me."

Through her lifelong dedication to education and wellness, she is considered a role model, especially to young black women. Her four initiatives as First Lady were created to inspire and motivate others, especially women, to seek higher education, be granted equal access to higher education and to live healthier lifestyle with a focus on healthier foods and exercise.

Role models motivate and inspire others to take some sort of action. Please describe your biggest role model and the ways that they have inspired or motivated you.

SONIA SOTOMAYOR

IMPORTANCE OF EXPERIENCE

"I would hope that a wise Latina woman with the richness of her life experiences would more often than not reach a better conclusion than a white male who hasn't lived that life."

Boy, this opinion stated by Sonya Sotomayor was criticized over and over and over again by conservatives and some Republicans during her nomination process. It was a line that she used in some form in a number of her speeches, especially in a Berkeley Law lecture in 2001. Some of these folks even called her a racist for saying this. All that she was saying was that one's life experiences would make anyone wiser about the things that they had to judge or give an opinion on. Because many of the Supreme Court judges had no experiences as "people of color", with living in poverty and being poor; that a old, wise Latina could in some cases make a better decision than someone who had no real experience in that situation. That is all that she was saying!

In the spaces below, please share YOUR opinion on this opinion by the Supreme Court Justice. Who do you think would be the wisest and better able to judge cases involving "regular" people who look like us? Let me know if you think that it's important for the Supreme Court to have people of color represented on it?

AN AFFIRMATIVE ACTION BABY

"With my academic achievement in high school I was accepted rather readily at Princeton and equally as fast at Yale, but my test scores were not comparable to that of my classmates. And that's been shown by statistics, there are reasons for that - there are cultural biases built into testing, and that was one of the motivations for the concept of affirmative action to try to balance out those effects. I am the perfect affirmative action baby."

Affirmative action is a topic that seems to stay in the news. It's hard to understand why they think the way that they do, but a lot of people don't believe in affirmative action and they think that it is unfair. The only thing that affirmative action did was to "even the playing field"; it made sure that black and brown adults and youth had access to higher education (college) and jobs by "putting slots aside for us and making it mandatory" that a certain number of us got into those colleges and careers. This was necessary because racism oftentimes resulted in our not being accepted into college or being hired for certain jobs. Because of affirmative action, Sonya Sotomayor was able to get into and succeed in college and reach her goal of being a judge.

On the next page, please share your opinions of affirmative action. Let me know if you think that its fair to "guarantee" a certain or minimum number of college and jobs for people who look like us. Let me know if you think that it's even needed.

I DIDN'T DO IT BY MYSELF

"I stand on the shoulders of countless people, yet there is one extraordinary person who is my life aspiration - that person is my mother, Celina Sotomayor."

This was a very humble statement from Sonya Sotomayor. It's a way of saying that no one accomplishes anything without the help, support and guidance of others. "I stand on the shoulders of countless people" was not said to describe what she had experienced in a gymnastic class in physical education. Instead, it meant that countless people had helped her get to where she was...the first Hispanic on the Supreme Court. And, the most important person to have helped her was her mother.

Even though they seem to drive us crazy some times, our mothers are always there to help, support and encourage us. In the spaces below, you are going to write a "thank you" letter to your mom for all that she has done to help you get to where you are today.

RED RIBBON WEEK
Enrique "Kiki" Camarena

WORTH REMEMBERING: MY LEGACY

Enrique Camarena' work as a DEA agent to stop drugs from crossing the border, coming into America and eventually reaching the hands of young people was dangerous work. Agent Camarena was dealing with very serious, ruthless, and deadly people involved in the drug trade. Yes, he understood the risks of his profession and knew that he could be killed if his identity was ever discovered. But, he believed in the importance of keeping America's kids *"drug free"*.

Agent Camarena received numerous awards while with the DEA, and after his death, he posthumously received the Administrator's Award of Honor, the highest award given by the organization. In Fresno, the DEA hosts a yearly golf tournament named after him. The nationwide annual Red Ribbon Week, which teaches youths to avoid drug use, was established in his memory.

To believe in something that much is truly admirable and to pay the ultimate price for your beliefs is the stuff that heroes are made of and remembered for.

Do you believe that it is important for kids like you to be *"drug free"*? Would you have taken the risks that Enrique Camarena took to try to prevent drugs from reaching the hands of young people like you? If you were to be remembered for what you did, or thought about doing, to keep drugs from young people, what would that be and how would you be remembered by friends and family?

Luis Miramontes

EXCEEDING EXPECTATIONS OF OTHERS

Chemistry is a branch of physical science that studies the composition, structure, properties and change of matter and atoms. If you've taken any science classes, you know how, or you can imagine, how difficult of a subject it is. For whatever reason, you can count on two hands the number of Latino and/or Mexican students that have careers in the field of chemical engineering. Yes, his parents wanted him to have a life better than theirs, but can you imagine how surprised they were that he became so interested in chemistry. Even though his parents needed him to work to help the family with its finances, they did not discourage him from his educational pursuits.

Despite being torn in two different directions, he continued with his studies, obtained several degrees and professor-related university positions, and at the young age of 26 was one of the key inventors of the oral contraceptive. He became known and acknowledged around the world for his work and invention. He definitely exceeded the expectations of his parents.

Like most parents, the parents of Luis E. Miramontes had extremely high expectations for him and they wanted him to have a life better than theirs. Despite whether of not you are interested in the sciences, your parents also have high expectations for you and they want to see you have a life equal to or greater than their life.

In the spaces below, describe the 'greatness" that lies in your future.

91

FROM HUMBLE BEGINNINGS

Regardless of where we live and the quality of our lives, we all have the potential of doing something noteworthy and having a great life for ourselves and our families. Look at basketball greats Michael Jordan, Magic Johnson, and Larry Bird; look at their humble beginnings…where they came from, their early childhood years and their rise to "elite status" – the best in the world.

The same can be said of Luis E. Miramontes. He was a Mexican chemist who is known for being the co-inventor of the oral contraceptive, aka, the birth control pill. In 1964, the contraceptive pill was chosen by the U.S. Department of Patents as one of the 40 registered more important inventions between 1794 and 1964. The name of Luis Miramontes appeared next to the names of Pasteur, Edison, Bell and the Wright brothers and others of equal status. It was included in the USA Inventors Hall of Fame. In 2004, the invention of Luis E. Miramontes was chosen as the 20th most important one of all the times by a group of engineers in the United Kingdom.

Similar to MJ, Magic and Larry Bird , Mr. Miramontes' rise to importance was even so much more remarkable because of his humble beginnings. Despite coming from a hardworking and poor family, he rose to greatness and is credited with having one of the world's greatest inventions. Yes, we don't come from the wealthiest of families and communities, but we still have the potential of being great, living great lives and doing something great.

FROM HUMBLE BEGINNINGS

It is important to many of us that our lives mean something and is of value and it is important to "leave our mark" on our family, community, on society and on the world. By being one of the only Mexican chemical engineers ever, Luis Miramontes 'left his mark" on future generations of Mexican scientist by being a mentor and role model that could be looked up to when things became difficult. Perhaps equally as important to some, his work as co-inventor of the oral contraceptive "left his mark" around the world and established his legacy worldwide.

The importance of his invention was that it reduced unintended pregnancies and abortions, and facilitated family planning/spacing of births. Effective contraception provided both health and social benefits to mothers and their children. According to worldwide estimates, some 600,000 women die each year of pregnancy-related causes, and 75,000 die following unsafe abortions. At least 200,000 of these maternal deaths are attributable to the failure or lack of contraceptive services. In addition to preventing mortality, effective contraception improves maternal health. Data from the well-controlled Intergenerational Panel

Study of Mothers and Children, a 31-year longitudinal survey of 1113 mother-child pairs, indicate that unwanted births can lead to major depression (postpartum depression), feelings of powerlessness, increased time pressures, and a reduction in overall physical health. Finally, effective contraception improves the social and economic role of women and enables them to participate in society fully.

The size of the "mark" that we leave is not the important thing; the important thing is that we do leave something with our family, community, society or world that shows that "we were here" and that we made a "small difference". In the spaces below, please think about your future years and the "mark" that you will leave.

The Re-Education of
CARTER G. WOODSON

MORE THAN TALK

The purpose of "real education", according to Woodson, was to "inspire people to live more abundantly, and to learn to begin with life as they find it and make it better." He felt that education should prepare and train us to not only recognize, complain about, and protest "undesirable conditions", but should also prepare us with the skills to develop constructive programs to address those same conditions. The education that Woodson saw black youth receiving prepared them to be complainers (malcontents), with no programs to offer for changing problem situations.

This drill requires you to think about one thing, or one problem, that you have strong opinions on, and have complained about. You are to describe that thing, or problem, and describe your "program" - what you would do to make that problem go away. Don't forget to include in your story what you will do to stop the problem; who will help you; how long it will take; whether or not it will be an easy or difficult task; what would happen if your program is successful; and what would happen if your program fails.

98

GIVING SOMETHING BACK

Carter G. Woodson was critical of black businessmen and black professionals who "did not give anything back" to their communities after they had become successful. He was really "hard" on these kinds of people because at
some stage of their life, some black people in their community saw their potential to succeed. Some one, or some ones, sacrificed their time and effort to motivate them to "keep on keeping on". However, once these people obtained their degrees, or became successful, they seemed to "turn their back" on those people and that community that had assisted them.

They didn't come back to "the hood" to share their resources and knowledge
with the community. By not sharing their information and experiences, they were contributing to the death of the very community which had inspired them on. In his opinion, "Returning and giving something back to one's
community is vital and is a prerequisite for our survival as a race".

This drill asks you to look at your long term goals and career aspirations and what you would like to accomplish educationally and professionally. When you reach your educational and professional goals, what kinds of skills, resources, or information can you give back to your community that might make it a little better for those youth who will follow you? How do you think that other young people and your community will be effected by what you do or don't do?

The Persistence of
IDA B. WELLS

Mightier Than the Sword

Ida B. Wells was a very determined and insightful black woman. She was very much aware of the power of the press in trying to combat many of the injustices received by black people in America. She realized that the press (newspapers, magazines, articles, etc.) was the way of giving people knowledge and making them more aware of some of the cruelties suffered by black people. She believed that if white people received the facts, their conscience would be effected, and they would put an end to their excessively cruel and inhumane treatment of blacks.

She devoted her life to using her journalistic skills to expose crime and injustice - particularly the facts regarding the lynching of innocent blacks in the South. Ida B. Wells understood the old saying that the "pen is mightier than the sword".

This is a difficult assignment that will require some thought. For this assignment, you are to share your opinion of what is meant by the expression, "the pen is mightier than the sword". In the spaces below, try to think of a situation that you may have experienced in which the "pen proved to be more powerful than the sword."

The Journalistic Me

Ida B. Wells was perhaps the **most famous black female journalist of her time**. She was a correspondent for the **Detroit Plain Dealer**, the **Christian Index**, the **People's Choice**, and had written for several publications, including the **New York Age**, the **Indianapolis World**, the **Little Rock Sun**, the **Memphis Watchman**, and the **Fisk Herald**. She was also a columnist for **Our Women Of Color**. Her many articles were directed at the American conscience and attempted to get it to come to grips with its treatment of black people, particularly the attacking and lynching of innocent black people.

Many of us either are good writers, or enjoy writing. A few of us have been lucky enough to have written articles for our school, or neighborhood, newspapers. This activity requires you to write a story (or article) about someone, or something going on at your school that might be interesting to your fellow schoolmates. Your story should include all of the important details that would be important for your fellow students to know.

To Bug Or Not To Bug: When I Get On Someone's Nerve

Ida B. Wells bugged and "irritated the nerves" of many people. Of course, those who were irritated most by Ms. Wells were Southern whites; those same Southern whites who were actively involved in the brutality and lynching of innocent black people. These people got so irritated that they defaced and destroyed her newspaper office and printing equipment. If they had known that the writer of all of the "lynching articles" was Ms. Wells - she was using the pen name of Iola - they would have probably tried to murder her also. Ms. Wells' constant bugging proved to be successful. She was able to touch the conscience of enough people that a law was passed outlawing the lynching of black people.

We all know when we are bugging someone and are getting on their nerve. We know all of the little ways to annoy our friends, parents, and teachers. For today's assignment, you are going to describe a time when you really bugged someone. I want to know what you did and who you did it to. Tell me how people react to you bugging them.

Words to Remember

As a journalist, Ida B. Wells was skilled in using the English language to her advantage. She was able to increase people's awareness of the conditions being faced by black people, and was able to make "good" white people feel guilty about some of the actions of other whites in the South. The words listed below are associated with the life and contributions of Ms. Wells. In your spare time, look them up, and use them in a sentence.

1. Vandalism:

_____

_____

_____

2. Lynching:

_____

_____

_____

3. Injustice:

_____

_____

4. Deface:

_____

_____

5. Correspondent:

_____

_____

_____

6. Obstacle:

_____

_____

_____

7. Relentless:

_____

_____

Staff Feedback

_____

_____

_____

_____

ALEXANDRIA OCASIO-CORTES

"We Can be Whatever we Have the Courage to Be."

In 2019, at the young age of 29, Alexandria Ocasio-Cortez, a young Puerto Rican woman was elected to Congress to represent her New York City district. Her rise to Congress seemed like a fairy tale; from school to working with children to waiting tables to winning the primary for

Congress. She would say, "just imagine the talents the world has missed out by all of those people who weren't able to pursue their dreams." One can only imagine the determination and courage you need to have to overcome so many of life's challenges in to get that far in such a short amount of time.

Everyone has special talents and dreams for the future. Everyone will need to have the courage and the determination to confront the challenges that you will have to face to make your dreams come true. In the spaces below, describe what great things are part of your future, some of the obstacles that might stand in the way, and how you will overcome them.

I Am a Descendant of All Sorts of Folks.

Ocasio-Cortez is Nuyorican (a person of Puerto Rican-descent, born and raised in New York). In an interview, she talked about her heritage citing: "My identity is the descendant of many different identities. I am the descendant of African slaves. I am the descendant of Indigenous people. i am the descendant of Spanish colonizers... I am a descendant of all sorts folks.

Have you ever thought about all of the different descendants that you come from. Yes, we all have ancestry that can be traced back to Africa, the home of the first "human being". But, since that time, humans have been traveling, mingling and evolving and our heritage is a mix of different ethnicities. In the spaces below, describe all of the ethnic groups of your descendants.

"I was born in a place where your ZIP code determines your destiny."

Alexandria Ocasio-Cortez (AOC) has proven that anyone can get anywhere. AOC was born in the neglected community of the South Bronx and so did her father. Her mother was born in Puerto Rico and was a school bus driver and house cleaner. Earlier in her life, she had worked as a waitress and bartender to make ends meet. She once said, "Women like me aren't supposed to run for office." Because of that belief, she connected at a deeper level to her black and brown constituents. Alexandria Ocasio-Cortez –at the age of 29-is the youngest woman ever to be elected to the US Congress.

Unfortunately, many of us are still judged by the "zip code" of our neighborhood and the community where we were raised; people see certain zip codes and "stereotype" us. AOC was a able to prove these people wrong as she rose to become a congresswoman in 2019. So what does your zip code say about you and what will you do in the future to prove these the haters wrong.

Made in the USA
Columbia, SC
15 October 2024

44136893R00076